AF261229
VAN GOGH ALMOND BLOSSOMS
12 SHEETS SINGLE-SIDED
SCRAPBOOKING DESIGNS FOR CRAFTS
SCRAPBOOK PAPER PAD
6x6, NON-PERFORATED SHEETS
© Crafty As Ever

To remove cut along the dotted line.

To remove cut along the dotted line.

TO REMOVE CUT ALONG THE DOTTED LINE.

TO REMOVE CUT ALONG THE DOTTED LINE.

To remove cut along the dotted line.

TO REMOVE CUT ALONG THE DOTTED LINE.

TO REMOVE CUT ALONG THE DOTTED LINE.

TO REMOVE CUT ALONG THE DOTTED LINE.

TO REMOVE CUT ALONG THE DOTTED LINE.

TO REMOVE CUT ALONG THE DOTTED LINE.

To remove cut along the dotted line.

TO REMOVE CUT ALONG THE DOTTED LINE.

www.ingramcontent.com/pod-product-compliance
Lightning Source LLC
Chambersburg PA
CBHW042141030726
47599CB00002B/573